D1443625

HEALTH CARE CAREERS IN 2 YEARS™

JUMP-STARTING CAREERS AS

MEDICAL ASSISTANTS & CERTIFIED NURSING ASSISTANTS

JENNIFER CULP

ROSEN
PUBLISHING®

New York

Published in 2014 by The Rosen Publishing Group, Inc.
29 East 21st Street, New York, NY 10010

Copyright © 2014 by The Rosen Publishing Group, Inc.

First Edition

Library of Congress Cataloging-in-Publication Data

Culp, Jennifer.
Jump-starting careers as medical assistants & certified nursing assistants
/Jennifer Culp. — First edition.
    pages cm. — (Health care careers in 2 years)
Includes bibliographical references and index.
ISBN 978-1-4777-1697-7 (library binding)
1. Medical assistants—Vocational guidance. 2. Nurses' aides—Vocational
guidance. 3. Medical offices—Management—Vocational guidance. I. Title.
R728.8.C85 2013
610.73'7069—dc23

                                                                2013013846

Manufactured in Malaysia

CPSIA Compliance Information: Batch #W14YA: For further information, contact Rosen Publishing, New York, New York, at
1-800-237-9932.

CONTENTS

At 7:30 AM, Bridget arrives to open the office before the first patient's appointment at 8:00. She starts a pot of coffee to offer early patients, then sits down to check her e-mail. The practice's physician comes in to say hello on his way in. Bridget makes sure the day's patient files are in order according to the schedule, and then it's time to check in a patient for the first appointment. This is a repeat patient Bridget knows well. She takes his I.D., insurance cards, and paperwork and logs in to the computer system to make sure that his information is recorded correctly. If he were a new patient, she would enter all of his data into the system. When she is sure that everything is in order, she marks that he has been checked in electronically and takes his file to the physician, who calls him back to begin the appointment. Bridget returns to her desk and calls another patient to discuss the results of laboratory work that was ordered during her last appointment. When the doctor is finished seeing the first patient of the day, Bridget logs back in to the computer system to schedule a follow-up appointment; the physician wants to see the patient again in three weeks. She makes a joke to the patient, who has visited the office several times in the past year, and sends him off with a smile. She will check patients in and out, take payments, schedule follow-up appointments, and answer the phone throughout

A medical assistant helps a patient fill out his paperwork correctly before he sees the doctor. Keeping accurate records is vitally important to a medical practice.

the day. Today, lunchtime is a treat: a representative from a drug company takes the staff out to eat and tells them about a new medication that can help with a common condition among the practice's patients. In the afternoon, Bridget fills out paperwork and calls an insurance company to obtain a prior authorization for a treatment a patient needs. When that is accomplished, she retrieves the physician's audio notes, puts on headphones, and transcribes reports of the morning's appointments. She gathers the billing sheets and stores them in an orderly file to process at the end of the week, when she will also enter the staff's time sheets into the computer system and authorize payroll. Before leaving at the end of the day, she makes a note to remind herself to work on the office's newsletter, which is scheduled to be e-mailed to patients at the end of the week.

Three hours later on the other side of town, Heather begins an overnight shift at the community hospital. She checks the list of patients she is assigned to care for and then heads to the first patient's room to make sure he is comfortable. Throughout the first half of the night she helps the nurses with tasks as needed and assists some of the patients when they need to visit the restroom. Around 2:00 AM, she spends some time sitting with an elderly woman who feels scared and can't sleep. The woman asks if Heather will sing a hymn from her childhood with her. Heather sings three verses of the song with the patient, who is then able to relax and go to sleep. As morning nears, Heather helps bathe several patients and, along with a nurse, assembles a lifted scale to weigh an immobilized patient. Heather is responsible for phlebotomy duties, so she draws, collects, and sends morning blood specimens for all of the patients on her floor to the laboratory. As the last duty of her shift, she bags up the laundry, trash, and sharp containers before she checks out for the day.

Bridget is a medical assistant. Heather is a certified nursing assistant. Both women have challenging jobs with a great deal of variety; neither knows exactly what her workday will entail when she arrives. At the end of their respective workdays, both Bridget and Heather leave with satisfaction. They know that they have done important work and have made a positive impact in patients' lives.

Chapter 1

What Is a Medical Assistant?

When you get sick and need medical care, you "go to the doctor" to get well. That phrase isn't really accurate, though. A trip to see the doctor isn't *just* a visit to a physician but to his or her whole office and staff. Despite long years of expensive education and training, doctors and nurses can't provide the very highest level of patient care without help. That's where unlicensed medical assistive personnel, such as medical assistants and nurses' aides, come in.

Although the terminology may seem confusing at first, the term "medical assistant" should not be confused with "physician assistant," which is an entirely separate career. Physician assistants, who are also known as PAs, must complete a bachelor's degree and graduate-equivalent level accredited program before becoming licensed to practice medicine under the supervision of physicians and surgeons. The terms "medical assistant" and "medical assistive personnel" encompass a wide variety of jobs that do not initially require formal education beyond a high school diploma.

The hard work of medical assistants and certified nursing assistants helps to provide patients with better care. Medical assistants and nursing aides work in all types of medical practice, everything from pediatrics to podiatry!

Responsibilities

Depending on the state in which a medical assistant works, office size and the individual practice in which he or she works, and specialization of the medical assistant, responsibilities may vary widely. Medical assistants complete administrative and clinical tasks in outpatient physicians' offices, hospitals, surgical practices, nursing homes, and other health care facilities. At any given doctor's office visit, you probably see several medical

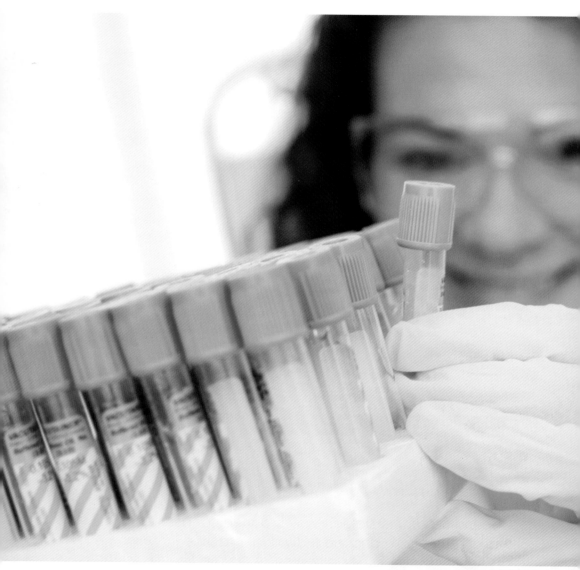

Some medical assistants focus on administrative duties, while others work in the clinical side of practice. These medical assistants take vital signs, prepare patients for laboratory tests, and may even draw blood.

assistants. The job is often a mix of office work and clinical duties. Office work can include answering the phone, greeting incoming patients, scheduling appointments, and organizing insurance forms and patient records. Clinical duties consist of taking patients' histories and vital signs, sterilizing surgical equipment, preparing blood for laboratory tests, helping doctors and nurses with patient examinations, and even drawing blood and giving injections. Across the board, medical assistants are important members of any health care delivery team. They are essential to all aspects of a practice, including the examining room, administrative office, and laboratory, and act as an important liaison between doctors and patients.

Likewise, nurses' aides are vitally important to health care facilities.

SCOPE OF PRACTICE, MEDICAL ASSISTANT

The duties a medical assistant is allowed and expected to undertake vary between states and medical facilities. While aspiring medical assistive personnel must check the guidelines set out by their own place of residence and employment in order to learn specifics, the list below presents common responsibilities included in a medical assistant's scope of practice.

- Work in reception
- Answer telephone
- Schedule appointments
- Process medical billing
- Keep financial records
- File medical charts
- Telephone prescriptions to a pharmacy
- Transcribe dictation
- Send letters
- Manage accounts payable
- Process payroll
- Document and maintain accounting and banking records
- Develop and maintain fee schedules
- Perform office personnel management functions
- Negotiate leases and prices for equipment and supply contracts

- Carry out patient history interviews
- Take and record vital signs
- Prepare patients for examination
- Provide patient information and instructions
- Assist with medical examinations and/or surgical procedures
- Set up and clean patient rooms
- Maintain inventory and restock supplies
- Notify patients of laboratory results
- Translate during medical interviews with non-English-speaking patients
- Give prevention reminders
- Instruct patients about medications or special diets
- Develop educational materials
- Educate patients about procedures
- Prepare medications as directed
- Change dressings
- Perform basic laboratory tests
- Perform venipuncture (draw blood)
- Administer immunizations
- Collect and prepare laboratory specimens
- Remove sutures (stitches)

—Adapted from the American Association of Medical Assistants Role Delineation Study

Nurses' aides provide basic care and assistance with patients' daily living activities in hospitals, nursing homes, and hospice facilities, or even travel to the homes of disabled or elderly patients to provide care. They monitor patients' vital signs (such as blood pressure and temperature), record patient concerns and progress, serve meals and help patients eat, assist patients with basic hygienic activities, and help transfer patients from place to place. Nurses' aides also clean and sterilize medical facilities and equipment, and in some states, they may dispense medication. Nurses' aides who work in nursing homes or who travel to visit homebound patients may develop close, affectionate relationships with the people they care for.

Training

Nurses' aides typically need to earn a postsecondary certificate and pass a competency exam after earning a high school diploma or passing a General Educational Development (GED) test. Passing a state-required competency exam allows nurses' aides to use state-specific titles. Because of these requirements, the term "nurses' aide" is relatively uncommon in this day and age. Now, they are most often called CNAs, for certified nursing assistants. CNA requirements vary from state to state, and CNAs

Certified nursing assistants help sick or disabled patients manage activities of daily living with dignity. Many CNAs develop affectionate relationships with the patients under their care.

must be placed on a state-specific registry in order to work in nursing homes and long-term-care facilities. Some states offer additional credentials beyond a CNA, such as an added certification, which allows the titleholder to give medications. CNAs work closely with nurses and are often a first line of communication with patients.

In addition to their other responsibilities, certified nursing assistants are often called upon to provide support and reassurance for patients who are nervous, scared, or confused.

Formal training is not required for medical assistants; however, it is strongly recommended and makes a candidate more competitive for job openings and higher pay. Without formal training, a medical assistant may not become eligible for certification until years of experience have been completed. Accredited postsecondary educational programs speed this process significantly, usually lasting for about one year and resulting in a certificate or diploma, or two years with an associate's degree. Most accredited programs also include an internship period, which offers an aspiring medical assistant practical on-the-job experience in an appropriate health care facility. Certification is not required for medical assistants, but many states require education and testing before allowing them to perform certain duties, such as taking X-rays, drawing blood, or giving injections. Employers typically prefer applicants who have passed a competency examination administered by a national medical assistant certification program.

As mentioned, medical assistants work in administrative and clinical aspects of a practice. In smaller offices, a medical assistant may generalize and do both. Larger health care facilities allow for specialization in various areas. Administrative medical assistants perform reception duties, organize and file patient data, and collect insurance information. These assistants schedule appointments, check patients in and out of the office, and may be responsible for buying and storing supplies and equipment for the practice or managing the practice payroll. An assistant who enjoys working in this area may become certified as a medical administrative specialist, advance to become an office or practice

SCOPE OF PRACTICE, CERTIFIED NURSING ASSISTANT

Though the responsibilities of certified nursing assistants differ somewhat by location, they tend to be more similar than those of medical assistants, focusing on providing basic care for incapacitated patients. The list below presents a number of typical CNA duties.

- Take and record vital signs:
  Blood pressure, pulse, temperature, respiration

- Measure and record statistics:
  Height, weight, intake and output

- Obtain routine lab samples not requiring laboratory personnel

- Help patients with activities of daily living:
  Bathing, combing hair, brushing teeth, shaving, dressing, ambulation (walking), using the restroom, eating and drinking

- Help patients with equipment for treatment (such as anti-embolism stockings, bladder scanner, intermittent pneumatic compression devices, and more)

- Patient transportation

- Infection control

- Observation and reporting on patient conditions

- Removal of potential hazards

- Clean patient environment and bedding

- Provide patient hydration

- Train and assist patients with range-of-motion exercises

- Ensure patient comfort

- Assess and tend to patient privacy needs

- Facilitate effective communication between patients and nurses

—Adapted from the Certified Nursing Assistant Certification Programs Guide

manager, and even teach medical assisting courses after gaining experience.

The responsibilities of clinically focused medical assistants vary widely by state and practice. A certified phlebotomist assistant is trained to draw blood from patients, requiring familiarity with the proper procedures to ensure that the blood-drawing equipment and environment are sterile and that each blood sample is documented. Medical laboratory technicians may also draw blood, collect samples, and perform tests to analyze body fluids and tissue. Surgical technologists (also known as operating room technicians) prepare for surgery by sterilizing operating rooms and equipment, washing and disinfecting incision sites, positioning patients for surgery, passing instruments to surgeons during an operation, handling specimens, applying dressings, and transporting patients.

Other medical assistants specialize even further, working in a specialty, rather than general, practice. Podiatric medical assistants, for example, work with physicians specializing in treating the foot, ankle, and lower leg. While the administrative duties of this assistant may resemble those of a more general practice, a podiatric medical assistant may be called upon to take and develop X-rays of a patient's feet and lower legs, make casts for orthotics, apply fiberglass casts for broken bones in the appropriate area, assist with minor foot surgeries, and even help with tests such as diabetic foot exams. Optometric and ophthalmic assistants work with the human eye, testing ocular functions with basic color vision and visual acuity trials, verifying eyeglass prescriptions, taking eye measurements with specialized equipment, administering topical ophthalmic medications, and training patients in how to insert contact lenses and care for eyewear. Outside of administrative functions, podiatric and ophthalmic assistants' jobs have very little in common. This holds true for the duties of clinical medical assistants working in most any highly specialized area of medicine. Responsibilities of CNAs also vary somewhat from practice to practice, but nurses' aides are more commonly focused on providing basic care rather than specialty-specific duties.

Regardless of specialty, the importance of medical assistants and CNAs in health care facilities cannot be overstated. According to *Family Practice Medicine*, the American Academy of Family Physicians' practice management journal, the contributions of medical assistants optimize office flow, allowing physicians to see more patients and accomplish more during visits. Medical assistants improve patient experience as well, providing one-on-one explanations of lab results and health conditions, making follow-up phone calls to patients, and

Compassion toward others in need is an important qualification in an aspiring medical assistant or certified nursing assistant. A friendly attitude helps cement good relationships with patients and other medical personnel.

generally maximizing patient/doctor communication. CNAs are also essential to the maintenance of patient well-being. Without the efforts of CNAs, ill or indisposed patients would not be able to carry out activities of daily living, such as bathing, grooming, and dressing themselves. CNAs speed the recovery process by assisting patients with active and passive range-of-motion exercises. In addition to providing necessary basic care, CNAs help patients maintain a sense of dignity and connection to the human side of healing.

Ultimately, the work of medical assistants and CNAs is beneficial to everyone: doctors and nurses, who can better allocate their own time and expertise thanks to the benefit of assistance; patients, who not only receive better care from physicians and nurses but benefit from personal interaction with medical assistive personnel; and medical assistants and CNAs themselves, who participate in challenging, rewarding work that truly makes a positive difference in the quality of health care.

Chapter 2

An Appealing Career

Many factors recommend medical assisting or certified nursing assisting as attractive career options. Working as a medical assistant or CNA is widely considered to be personally fulfilling. Medical assistants and CNAs provide a vital service that improves the quality of people's lives. These workers contribute to patients' well-being not only by performing their own duties but also by allowing doctors and nurses to see more patients and provide better overall care. The hard work of CNAs and medical assistants benefits the entire medical field. In return, CNAs and medical assistants benefit from interacting with patients and other medical professionals.

CNAs work closely with patients who are often elderly or disabled, helping them to perform necessary activities for daily living. Unlike the experience of interacting with the public while working in a restaurant or retail store, CNAs provide essential care for those they serve and often form close relationships with the patients under their care. Providing such valuable service can boost self-esteem and offer a sense of satisfaction. Data collection from the

Certified nursing assistants who work in long-term-care facilities see the same patients every day. Older patients in nursing homes have many interesting stories to tell and appreciate spending time with CNAs.

Center for Health and Care Work at the University of Pittsburgh shows that, on the whole, CNAs derive emotional satisfaction from their jobs and that most CNAs feel that they provide much-needed service to patients under their care. The same investigation revealed that many CNAs value the ability to "craft" their jobs in accordance with their personal preferences, developing personal relationships with residents and accessing extra resources in order to provide patients with dignity and comfort. These factors contributed greatly to job satisfaction. Eighty-two percent of the CNAs surveyed said they looked forward to coming to work, 80 percent reported strong loyalty toward their jobs, and more than 90 percent said that they feel their work makes the world a better place. These figures are supported by the statements

WHY I LOVE MY JOB

MARY, MEDICAL ASSISTANT

"I love the people I work with! I enjoy learning about the 'medical field,' as I've had no formal education in medicine, and find it fascinating. I also enjoy talking to most of our patients. It's interesting to learn about their lives and the other interests they have. Some patients have become real friends, which makes it pleasant when they call for an appointment."

RODNEY, CNA

"Interaction with the patients who are cognizant enough to chat—you get to hear their stories of the war, their families, and their lives before living in the nursing home."

GINA, MEDICAL ASSISTANT

"Dealing with the patients. You are the liaison between the patient and their physician, and an integral part of the patient's care team. Knowing that I'm part of a patient's well-being is the most rewarding part of the job."

KAREN, CNA

"To be privileged to be bedside (and it truly is a privilege) when someone passes was a life-changing experience that helped me to see my life much more clearly and learn what was truly important in life. I stopped working for Hospice in 2011, and it is those moments in my career that I miss the most. The best part of the experience for me was knowing that I met truly amazing people who needed assistance to make it through that most trying of times, and left them in a better way than when I first arrived."

SHANNA, MEDICAL ASSISTANT

"My job involves a lot of 'undercover' work that goes unseen, but I truly enjoy my work. And every now and then, I get a chance to help someone, and that is always a little reward for a tough day at work. I also enjoy my knowledgeable coworkers, who are always willing to help for the benefit of the patient."

CANDICE, CNA

"My very favorite part of my job is seeing the light in my residents' faces when I arrive. They appreciate you so much. Many of the people in the nursing home have no one close in their lives. We are the only ones that they see regularly, and there is a strong bond between me and my residents."

of individual CNAs. "Working with elderly and disabled people can be demanding," says Justin, a CNA in home health, "but it makes me feel good to help people in need. I provide a valuable service; my work improves patients' lives."

Job satisfaction among medical assistants is high, too. Medical assistant was ranked number four in health care careers on the *U.S. News & World Report's* "50 Best Jobs for 2012" list and remained within the top twenty recommendations in the same publication's list for 2013. Medical assistants do not work with patients as intimately as CNAs do but may still form relationships with regular patients over time. Medical assistants often form close bonds with the physicians for whom they serve as liaisons as well.

Work Hours and Schedule

Working as a medical assistant is usually a full-time job with regular scheduled hours. Since unlicensed assistants are not typically called upon to work in an emergency capacity, this means that medical assistants' work schedules are usually regular and predictable—no surprise extra shifts, calls on weekends, or other demands that might inconvenience a medical assistant outside of work hours. Some medical assistants work evenings and weekends for facilities that stay open full-time, but rarely in an emergency capacity. In the course of a regular workday, however, duties may vary widely. Medical assistants are often called upon to learn new skills or apply their knowledge in novel ways. The regular work schedule provides stability, while the changing task load prevents boredom on the job, resulting in high job

Medical assistants report a high level of satisfaction with their jobs. Though work hours are regular, new situations arise to test their skills and impart knowledge every day.

satisfaction among medical assistants. Lindy, who worked as a clinical medical assistant for five years before going to school to obtain a degree in the mental health field, said of her time as a medical assistant, "The thing that kept me in the job for longer than I intended was the wide variety of tasks I could invest my time in. I was never bored because there was always some other kind of thing to do. There was also a great sense of freedom and respect from my coworkers; my opinion was valued, and my understanding of patient information was appreciated."

Job Availability

Furthermore, job opportunities for both medical assistants and CNAs remain widely available, even in depressed economic climates. In fact, opportunities for medical assistants and CNAs are expanding. According to the United States Department of Labor, employment of medical assistants is expected to grow at a much faster rate than other occupations: by 31 percent between 2010 to 2020. Employment of CNAs is also expected to grow by an estimated 20 percent from 2010 to 2020. As preventative health care demands increase, medical practices grow and the need for medical assistants and CNAs rises. Job prospects for medical assistants are on the rise due in part to the aging baby boomer population; as the demand for preventative primary care rises and practices struggle to accommodate more patients, medical assistants are needed to handle both clinical and administrative duties. Even further demand for medical assistants is expected due to the widespread implementation of EHR (electronic health record) in medical practice. EHR has changed the nature of daily tasks in medical practices substantially and requires familiarity and comfort with computer technology. The Bureau of Labor Statistics shows that in 2010, there were about 527,600 medical assistant jobs in the United States. In February 2013, *U.S. News & World Report* estimated that 162,900 additional new job openings for medical assistants will become available over the course of the year. Many entry-level positions in other fields are highly competitive, and applicants may spend considerable time and expense on education and training only to find themselves

There is a rising need for medical assistants and CNAs in the United States. Busy medical practices need staffers to accommodate growing patient populations, opening up job opportunities for qualified individuals.

without a job. The high demand for medical assistants and CNAs, however, ensures that there is no shortage of positions for qualifying candidates.

Such widespread job availability becomes even more attractive when considering the education and training requirements for medical assistants and CNAs. In most states there are no formal educational requirements in place in order to become a medical assistant, and training may take place on the job. A high school diploma or equivalent is usually necessary in order to be hired as a medical assistant, and employers may prefer candidates who have undergone a training program and earned a certificate, particularly in the case of clinical medical assistants. Training programs available at community colleges, vocational schools, technical schools, or universities usually take about one year to complete. Some institutions offer more advanced two-year programs that lead to an associate's degree. It is not mandatory for a medical assistant to incur the expense of a traditional four-year bachelor's degree in order to begin his or her career. (Certification, which can improve a candidate's chances of being hired, will be discussed in more detail later.) According to the Bureau of Labor Statistics, as of May 2010 the top earning 10 percent of medical

It takes a relatively short amount of time to complete certified nursing assistant or medical assistant training in comparison to obtaining a four-year university degree, and costs much less.

assistants earned more than $40,000 annually. (Current salary figures may always be checked on the Bureau of Labor's Web site.)

CNAs, on the other hand, must not only earn a high school diploma but must also complete a postsecondary certification in order to work. (Hence the name "certified nursing assistant.") These programs are usually held by community colleges, vocational or technical schools, and medical facilities, and typically take six to twelve weeks to complete. The American Red Cross also offers CNA courses at low cost. Some medical facilities will actually cover the cost of training for aspiring CNAs, provided they work for the facility after successfully completing their certification. Following training, a potential CNA must pass a certification examination. Training requirements and examinations vary from state to state and can be checked on most states' health department Web sites. The top earning 10 percent of nursing aides, orderlies, and attendants earned an annual wage of more than $34,500 as of May 2010. (Current earnings may be checked online with the Bureau of Labor.)

When asked, several medical assistants and CNAs said that the demands of their jobs benefited them in lasting ways. "The most important skill I developed was patience with others," said Gail, a former CNA. "It is impossible to work in a situation where you care for people in that close and intimate a situation without mastering the art of being incredibly patient. However, you also learn that the patience is worth it—the rewards for being able to help someone, no matter the amount of effort you have put into it, are well worth the sacrifice."

Chapter 3

Training Requirements and Certification

E ducation and training requirements for becoming a certified nursing assistant or medical assistant vary by state. Check the Web site for your state's department of health in order to learn the specific requirements for practicing in your place of residence. A general overview of the process will be discussed in the following sections.

CNA Certification

Education and certification is required to work as a CNA. Working closely with sick, elderly, or disabled patients is a big responsibility, and CNA training helps to ensure that tasks are carried out properly.

Most CNA educational programs take somewhere from six to twelve weeks to complete and include classroom, skills labs, and hands-on clinical experience. Courses are taught by registered nurses (RNs) or licensed practical nurses (LPNs), who work closely with CNAs and are experts on the requirements of the job. After completing a certified nursing assistant course, a

A certified nursing assistant must undergo a training program and successfully complete an exam in order to become licensed to work in his or her state of residence.

prospective CNA must take the certification exam for the state in which he or she wishes to work. The CNA Certification Exam, also known as the National Nurse Aide Assessment Program, is designed to test the knowledge, skills, and abilities required in order to safely perform the duties of a certified nursing assistant. The examination consists of two parts: a written "classroom" test and a hands-on skills evaluation. Successful completion of the certification examination allows a CNA to be registered in his or her state of residence and become eligible for employment.

Once a CNA is licensed to work in one state, he or she may receive the right to work in another state by requesting what is known as reciprocity from the second state, basically meaning that the CNA asks the new state to recognize the approval received from the initial state. Some states have more stringent standards than others and may require that a CNA take extra classes or pass a new test to receive approval. A CNA may maintain approval in more than one state by continuing to work in both states and keeping documentation of employment. A certified nursing assistant must work at least one eight-hour shift every two years in order to maintain active certification. If a two-year period with no relevant employment passes, CNA certification will expire and the former CNA will require training and successful completion of a state examination in order to renew.

Medical Assistant Certification

Though there are no legal educational requirements for aspiring medical assistants, training and certification is highly recommended. Employers are far more likely to hire a candidate who has undergone classes and/or a clinical internship, rather than someone who has earned

Earning a high school diploma is not legally required but is very beneficial to an aspiring medical assistant. Studying hard is good preparation for medical assistant or CNA training.

a high school diploma but possesses no experience in the field. According to the American Association of Medical Assistants (AAMA), there are a number of reasons why a practice would prefer to hire a certified medical assistant, not only for the obvious reason of preferring a more experienced candidate. Hiring certified medical assistants is looked upon favorably by the National Committee for Quality Assurance and Joint Commission on Accreditation of Healthcare Organizations and helps to protect practices in the case of litigation. Certified medical assistants are preferred by the directors of managed care organizations due to cost limitations and the need for highly skilled, versatile employees. In fact, some employers may even require that their medical assistants be certified, though it is not mandatory according to current law.

Certification is usually achieved by taking a computer-based test, the CMA Certification Examination. This test is offered at scheduled times throughout the year by the American Association of Medical Assistants Certifying Board, in consultation with the National Board of Medical Examiners. Successfully completing the examination earns a medical assistant the CMA (AAMA) title and credential. In order to remain certified, a CMA (AAMA) medical assistant must renew the credential every sixty months, either by retaking the examination or earning sufficient continuing education credits through the AAMA or other accredited program (such as university or physician continuing medical education classes). The CMA Certification Examination tests for general medical knowledge such as terminology and anatomy, administrative knowledge such as management and insurance processing, and clinical knowledge such as patient preparation and pharmacology.

The examination questions are continually updated to reflect the evolving daily responsibilities of medical assistants in the field and developments in medical knowledge and technology. A properly accredited program will adequately prepare a hopeful CMA (AAMA) for the demands of the examination.

A medical assistant may choose to earn a different credential rather than CMA (AAMA). The American Medical Technologists (AMT) agency also offers certification for medical assistants. Those who successfully complete the AMT Certification Examination earn the title of registered medical assistant, or RMA. Applicants for RMA certification must either graduate from a medical assisting program accredited by CAAHEP or ABHES, like CMA applicants, or possess a minimum of five years experience working as a medical assistant before taking the exam. A medical assistant may also become designated as a national certified medical assistant (NCMA) through the National Center for Competency Testing. Like the RMA credential offered by AMT, those who wish to become NCMAs may qualify to take the examination either by graduating from an approved educational program or possessing qualifying work experience. NCCT requires that NCMAs complete a minimum of fourteen hours of approved continuing education each year in order to remain abreast of current knowledge and maintain their certification. Finally, a medical assistant may become a certified clinical medical assistant (CCMA) by taking the National Healthcareer Association's certification exam. In order to be eligible for NHA certification, a candidate must possess a high school diploma or GED, have completed a training program or have one year of

MY CNA TRAINING

Justin originally became a certified nursing assistant to help a loved one and later became a home health worker who travels to disabled and elderly people's homes to help them maintain normal lives. Here is his story.

When I was nineteen, my great-grandmother broke her hip and needed someone to take care of her. I went to live with her and underwent CNA training in order to help her out. I found a cost-effective CNA training program in my area and signed up.

The class took two months to complete. In the first section we studied how to take care of hospitalized people—move, ambulate, and transport people without hurting them, help them successfully complete activities of daily living (which we called ADLs), and assist them in maintaining good hygiene. We learned how to help a patient bathe (in bed and out) and shave, help them use the toilet, make a bed (with or without a patient in it), and take vital signs and blood pressure. We were taught about the importance of keeping elderly patients active to prevent them from mental and physical deterioration.

In the second half of the course we worked on practical knowledge. We learned how to apply the things we had learned from the book and interact with patients directly. It was difficult at times, but incredibly rewarding to see the positive effects my efforts produced for people who were unable to take care of themselves without help.

At the end of the training program, I took and passed the CNA examination for the state of Tennessee. The first section consisted of multiple-choice questions. On the following day, I had to go to a separate facility and take part in a practical demonstration. In order to pass, I had to show that I could correctly complete five out of twelve tasks that we had practiced. After I passed the test, I became eligible to work as a CNA in my state. I worked at the facility where I trained as a CNA and lived with and took care of my great-grandmother. Because of my training, I was able to help her stay mobile and work on her rehabilitation. It was really rewarding to be able to give back to someone who took care of me when I was young.

work experience in the field, and be at least eighteen years of age. NHA certification lasts for two years and may be maintained longer by earning continuing education credits.

None of these designations are superior to one another. Though the majority of certified medical assistants earn certification through AAMA's program, the CMA (AAMA), RMA, NCMA, and CCMA titles are all equally and highly respected and sought after by employers. Each of these designations proves a high level of knowledge, skill, and dedication to the field.

Before achieving any certification, however, a medical assistant or prospective medical assistant must meet the eligibility requirements for testing. Unless the candidate has already worked as a medical assistant for a number of years, thus earning experience in the field, successful completion of an educational program accredited by the Commission on Accreditation of Allied Health Education Programs (CAAHEP) or the Accrediting Bureau of Health Education Schools (ABHES) is required. Some certifications, such as CMA (AAMA), require graduation from a medical assisting training program regardless of experience in the field. Any prospective medical assistant who wishes to earn a CMA (AAMA) title should be careful to check that the training program he or she chooses is accredited by one of the two recognized organizations (CAAHEP and ABHES) before signing up. This might sound daunting initially, but these two agencies have accredited about seven hundred different medical assisting programs throughout the United States, making it relatively easy to find a program available locally. Fortunately, it's easy to determine whether a program is accredited by one of the two major accepted agencies. You can check to see whether a program is accredited by the CAAHEP or ABHES on their Web sites.

Medical assistant training programs that result in a certificate or diploma usually take about one year to complete, whereas the completion of an associate's degree takes around two years. Though each educational program will differ based on its teacher and curriculum, those accredited by CAAHEP or ABHES should prepare a candidate to pass a certification examination and earn the title of CMA (AAMA), RMA, NCMA, or CCMA.

Training programs typically include such material as medical terminology, anatomy, and physiology, and include classroom and laboratory portions. A high school background in biology and chemistry may be helpful but is not necessary in order to successfully complete a medical assistant educational program.

Professional Organizations

Joining a professional organization, such as the American Association of Medical Assistants or National Network of Career Nursing Assistants, can offer unique benefits. In addition to providing a network of peers to communicate with about job-related issues, a professional organization

Making connections with peers in the field can greatly benefit your career in health care. Professional organizations allow a medical assistant to network nationally as well as locally.

may assist with transfer of certification from one state to another, offer peer counseling and mentor support, and provide special educational opportunities and training sessions. The AAMA, as discussed previously, actually offers a special certification for medical assistants. Career associations can also help members attain needed qualifications and network to locate desired jobs.

Every organization is different and provides different services for members, and prospective members should take the time to determine which best fits their individual needs. An administrative medical assistant who plans to become the office manager of a practice might do better to join the Association for Healthcare Administrative Professionals, rather than a more broadly focused group. While researching professional organizations with intent to join, a person should consider not only his or her current position but the future work he or she would like to do.

Chapter 4

Landing a Job

As we've established, working as a medical assistant or certified nursing assistant can be a rewarding career and offers many benefits for a low initial investment of money and time. Opportunities to find work in the field abound. But just how should one go about getting a job as a CNA or medical assistant?

Where to Look

First things first: if you want to be hired to work as a medical assistant or certified nursing assistant, you have to find an available position. Where should you start looking?

Medical assistants work at all sorts of medical facilities: hospitals, family practice centers, small private practices, university-affiliated health centers, you name it. Scouting the "Careers" or "Jobs" tab of local medical facilities' Web sites is one of the best ways to discover new job openings. Remember to check often to avoid missing an opportunity. Job turnover is typically higher at

A good first impression is critical to getting hired for any job.
Keep track of your accomplishments, look out for job openings,
and maintain a positive attitude!

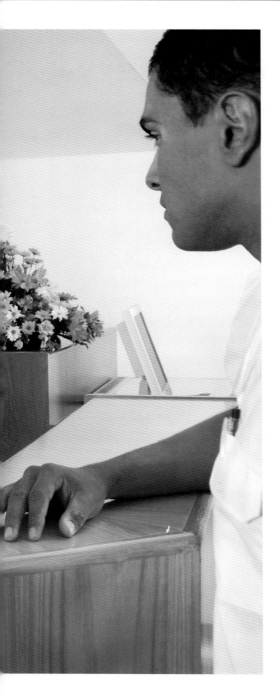

larger facilities with more jobs to offer, though this isn't always the case.

Here's where it gets a little tricky: practices looking to hire medical assistants often don't list the position simply as "medical assistant," but under other names more descriptive of the responsibilities specific to the position or practice. An administrative medical assistant position could be listed as "clerical assistant," "administrative assistant," or "receptionist." Don't immediately discount a potential job opening based on its title; always check the description to see what the facility's requirements are and what the job responsibilities actually entail. You might not have ever imagined yourself working as a "patient coordinator," only to find that your skills and training are perfectly suited for the job.

Many CNAs work in hospitals, nursing homes,

WRITING AN EFFECTIVE RÉSUMÉ

These days, the initial steps of hiring a new medical assistant or certified nursing assistant take place online, sight unseen. This allows hiring directors to winnow the pool down to the candidates they feel will be most appropriate for the job prior to scheduling interviews. Because of this, it is extremely important to maintain a professional résumé and garner strong positive recommendations from instructors, employers, and colleagues. A résumé should present your skills and qualifications clearly so that a future employer can determine that you are well suited for the job at a glance.

The first, most important thing a résumé should include is your full name and contact information: e-mail address, phone number, and physical address. Documentation of your accomplishments serves no purpose if an employer can't figure out who you are or contact you. Following your personal information, it is typical to include a brief statement summing up your positive qualities as an employee. For example, "Diligent, highly motivated certified nursing assistant. Enjoys interacting with patients; learns new skills quickly." This should be very to the point and give a hiring director a brief, positive picture of your potential as an employee of the organization.

Finally, the body of the résumé: it should be consistently formatted and easy to read. Items should be grouped under logical headings, like "Education" (including high school diploma or G.E.D., and any certification training), "Work Experience" (any jobs held), "Extracurricular Activities" (sports, clubs, volunteering, activities that demonstrate dedication and achievement), etc. List items in reverse chronological order, most recent at the top, older things underneath. If you make one heading bold, make them all bold. Don't use bullet points in one part of the résumé and neglect them in another. Making a résumé simple and nice to look at gives you a greater chance of catching a hiring director's eye.

As mentioned previously, include information to let a potential employer know exactly what your skills are. Did you graduate from a medical assistant educational program? Great! Include that item on your résumé. Consider including a line beneath it, however, to add such details as, "Completed anatomy and physiology course, participated in clinical internship at hospital, underwent training course in electronic health record system." This gives a much better understanding of your experience and value than merely including the fact that you completed an educational program. Be sure to keep these descriptions concise, however; a hiring director doesn't want to read a whole book about your training program. Do your best to present your qualifications and experiences in one page.

Continued on the following page

Continued from the previous page

It is very, very important that you double and triple check for spelling and grammatical errors in a résumé. Have a teacher (or two) look it over and check for mistakes. Errors in a résumé can make a candidate look sloppy or careless, and it would be a shame to lose out on a chance at a job over something as silly as a simple misspelling.

and hospice care facilities, or for home health organizations that send workers to provide care for disabled or homebound patients. Due to the large demand for certified nursing assistants, CNA turnover tends to be high, meaning the likelihood of finding an open position at any given time is good. Checking local facilities' Web sites or placing calls to their hiring directors will allow you to find out if any positions are currently available. Once again, remember to check the job description before discounting a listing with an unfamiliar name. Though some facilities may use unique, specific titles, the listed job requirements will always include CNA certification for a CNA position.

In addition to searching individual medical facilities' Web sites for job openings, résumé-sharing Web sites can prove helpful during a job search. Professional organizations for medical assistants and CNAs, such as the American Association of Medical Assistants, the National Association of Healthcare Assistants, and the National Network of Career Nursing Assistants provide resources for qualified job seekers.

Make a Good Impression

In order to earn a job, keep a job, or advance in the field, it is vital to show others that you are a good worker who can be trusted with responsibility. Making a good impression isn't just important in the middle of a job

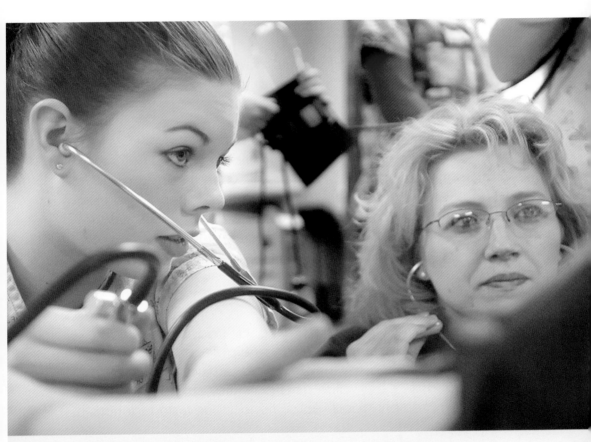

Teachers in medical assistant or certified nursing assistant training programs have valuable knowledge to impart. Aspiring job applicants in these fields should pay close attention!

interview, but throughout training, job seeking, and while on the job. The respect of the people you work with, under, and around—teachers, bosses, coworkers, etc.—is incredibly important when it comes to getting hired.

When it comes to impressing others with stellar performance, undergoing a training program and earning certification is a great place to start. As discussed previously, CNAs *have* to be certified, whereas certification is not required for medical assistants, but it is still preferable in the latter case. While taking part in an educational program, students get to know at least one respected individual who works in the field they hope to join: the teacher. Working hard and performing well in a CNA or medical assistant training course is a good way to earn an excellent letter of recommendation from the instructor. This can be particularly beneficial when it comes to getting hired for a position. A positive recommendation from someone who works in your desired field, who knows exactly what qualifications are required for the job, is likely to carry more weight with a potential employer than a letter from a high school teacher or even a previous employer. That's not to suggest that school or an after-school job aren't important places to demonstrate a good work ethic, however. Making good grades in science classes and being punctual and reliable at work are great ways for a young aspiring medical assistant or CNA to show off his or her value as a potential employee and can help cement good recommendations from teachers and employers.

Clinical portions of training are a great place to make valuable contacts in the field, too. Showing up on time, working diligently, being respectful to patients and colleagues, and presenting oneself in a clean, well-groomed fashion all make a positive impression on potential employers and coworkers. In fact, many medical assistants locate jobs through contacts they have made with people who work for a particular medical facility or group. Lindy, who worked as a medical assistant for a small specialty practice for five years, originally worked in an unrelated position in the same office. Her reliability and successful performance at other duties showed her employers that she could handle large responsibilities, and she eventually became head coordinator for the entire office. Mary, who works as an administrative medical assistant for a family medicine center, first obtained a job working in patient accounts, which she disliked. Her good performance at her tasks, however, benefited her when the clerical position she preferred opened up.

Teachers, coworkers, fellow students, and acquaintances who work in the field are all valuable allies when it comes to locating and securing a job. Having a "friend on the inside," so to speak, is a valuable source of information and support. An instructor who respects a would-be medical assistant's attitude and classwork might speak to that student privately and mention that a position at the instructor's medical practice has become available. Likewise, people who are already aware of a newly certified CNA's good work ethic may pass on positive unofficial "word-of-mouth" recommendations to a hiring director, boosting that particular candidate's chance of getting the job over other qualified individuals. Connections are important, and a smart aspiring medical assistant or

CNA remembers that every interaction with someone who works in the medical field is a chance to make a good impression.

Gain Experience, Then Show It Off

Like most employers, medical facilities on the lookout for new medical assistants and CNAs place a high value on a candidate's experience in the field. Proven experience with the skills and tasks required of a CNA or medical assistant is a no-brainer for a hiring director; if a person has already performed a similar job well, he or she will almost certainly be a good employee if hired. But how should a person go about gaining experience, especially if he or she is young and doesn't have an extensive work history? It can sound intimidating, but don't worry. There are a lot of ways to gain experience and show your worth as a future medical assistant or CNA.

Obviously, graduating from a training course is a great way to gain experience if you're starting from scratch. There are other ways to gain valuable experience that can help you secure a position as a medical assistant or CNA, too. Volunteering at a hospital not only immerses a potential medical employee in the environment he or she hopes to work in, but it is an important service and personally gratifying experience. Taking an elective anatomy class in high school can be helpful to prepare for future clinical work, and serving as a club officer demonstrates valuable organizational skills required for administrative work. Ask questions when you pay a visit to the doctor's office. Many facilities will allow you to schedule an appointment to "shadow" medical

Volunteering at a hospital can expose a potential medical assistant or certified nursing assistant to the facility and a wide variety of patients and procedures.

professionals at work, following them through their daily duties to see firsthand what the job is really like. All of these activities are helpful in preparing for a career as a medical assistant or CNA.

Gaining valuable experience in the field is only the first part of the equation, however. In order to be hired, a potential employee must demonstrate the fruits of that experience to his or her future boss. That can be one of the hardest tasks of all: *remembering* all of the good work you've done to put it on a résumé or tell a hiring director about it. Make a point to keep track of your accomplishments so that they can do you the most good. Keep a log of volunteer hours at the hospital, and write down the different tasks you assist with. Did you take an anatomy class? Don't just list the class on your résumé; include a brief summary of the material covered. What did you practice, specifically, in the clinical portion of your CNA training? Disinfecting surfaces, disposing of hazardous materials, how to safely help a patient stand up from a wheelchair? Make a list so that you can include specifics on your résumé. Including detail gives a hiring director a much better idea of the skills and abilities you possess. Don't expect your future boss to infer your accomplishments on his or her own; let the person know why you're the best candidate for the job.

Chapter 5

Expanding Horizons

Working as a medical assistant or certified nursing assistant offers many benefits, and both occupations are expected to grow significantly in the next decade. While this is largely due to the rising need for medical assistants and CNAs in growing practices, job openings for these positions also remain plentiful due to relatively high turnover in these occupations. Medical assistants and CNAs are essential to the day-to-day workings of a medical facility, and they learn a lot while they are on the job. Many medical assistants and CNAs take the knowledge and skills they acquire while working in these positions and apply themselves to move further up the hierarchy of the medical field, seeking even greater challenges.

Getting Certified

As discussed earlier, though many employers prefer certification, it is optional for medical assistants. Certain duties may require specialized certification, however, such as

There is always something interesting to learn on the job as a medical assistant or certified nursing assistant. Paying close attention can introduce new procedures and skills that may benefit your career.

drawing blood or taking X-rays. After entering the field as a general medical assistant, an individual may find that he or she feels more strongly drawn toward one area of practice than others. In this case, the assistant may wish to specialize in and focus on specific tasks that require a level of expertise beyond that of the general medical assistant. At this point, he or she could seek specialized certification in order to become a certified phlebotomist's assistant, an X-ray technician, a medical laboratory technician, or a surgical technologist. There are many options. A specialized assistive position, which requires specific training and/or certification, such as those listed, often offers higher pay than that of a general administrative or clinical medical assistant. Medical assistive personnel who find themselves interested in specific medical procedures or areas of medicine may wish to consider pursuing special certification in their area of interest or seeking employment in a specialized practice.

A medical assistant or certified nursing assistant who finds himself or herself interested in a certain area of medicine may continue training and education to focus on a particular interest, such as physical therapy.

The Value in Work Experience

Experience gained while working as a CNA or medical assistant can prove extremely valuable in other occupations. Gina, who worked as patient coordinator for a small specialty practice, leveraged her skills to earn a higher-paying, more prestigious position at a larger health clinic, where she works to help the clinic gain patient-centered care certification. "I gained valuable skills and knowledge while working as a medical assistant," Gina explained. "These skills are very marketable in the medical field. After working as a medical assistant, you would be qualified for positions such as a coding specialist or referral specialist. It can also give you the knowledge and experience to go further in health care by pursuing a nursing, or other health care, degree. For me personally, my medical assistant experience afforded me the opportunity to work for a health clinic to assist them in achieving a patient-centered care certification. I am developing processes and procedures to help the clinic run more efficiently and also making changes to the clinic's EHR system to fit the patient-centered model due to my medical background."

Rodney, who formerly worked in a nursing home and rehabilitation center, put the skills he acquired as a CNA to use in a related profession. "In my current job, I service and repair motorized and manual wheelchairs, often visiting patients in their homes to diagnose and make repairs," he said. "The skills I learned as a CNA help me to more effectively interact with patients and put them at ease."

ELECTRONIC HEALTH RECORDS AND THE CHANGING MEDICAL FIELD

The medical field exists in a near-constant state of change, evolving and adapting to best serve patients and provide quality health care. Given the last decade's advancements in technology, there is a widespread movement toward the implementation of electronic health records (EHRs) across medical organizations in the United States. Loosely, EHR means a digitally based record of health information about individual patients and populations that may, due to its digital nature, be shared across different health care settings. In practice, this means that much data that was once recorded on paper is now handled through a computer system. Patients are checked in on a computer, and their vital signs and statistics are recorded electronically rather than in a paper file. Doctors type their findings into a portable computer in the process of seeing a patient, instead of making audio notes to be transcribed later. Prescriptions and instructions are shared through the system, which may be accessed by any affiliated medical office the patient visits.

This method of storing and sharing information is intended to be efficient and effective for patients and health care providers. However, the process of implementing EHR is a huge task, requiring sweeping changes to activities on every level of a medical practice. Young employees who grew up accustomed to rapidly evolving technology are at an advantage in this environment, as employers must look to hire candidates who not only can cope with the responsibilities required of a medical assistant or CNA, but also successfully work with the facility's EHR system. Additionally, the push toward EHR has created a number of jobs for those who help medical offices transition to an EHR system and train employees in how to use it. Such occupations pay very competitively and are unlikely to disappear any time soon. Experience working as a medical assistant and using a local group's particular EHR system makes a candidate very competitive when it comes to hiring for EHR-related jobs.

As Gina pointed out, the skills medical assistants and CNAs gain in the course of working at their jobs and familiarity with the medical field open up a vast array of possibilities for those who are interested in seeking higher education in order to pursue degree-requiring careers. For example, a CNA may decide to go through nursing school and become a registered nurse or licensed practical nurse. CNAs work closely with nurses and are quite familiar with their duties and responsibilities. For an individual who enjoys working as a CNA and wishes to shoulder greater responsibility and earn higher pay, attending nursing school may be a logical progression.

Lindy, who worked as an administrative medical assistant for five years and advanced to become head coordinator of her practice, chose to go to college to earn a higher degree in the mental health field. Before working as a medical assistant, she had no intention of pursuing a career in the medical field. She discovered a passion for helping patients, however, and now finds that the work she did as a medical assistant benefits her current job as a therapist. "It is really helpful to have an inside look at how diagnosis, reimbursement, and follow-up works in the medical field," she said. "While there are significant differences in mental health, the general information I became familiar with as a medical assistant has helped; and I also have a much better understanding of how I can work in conjunction with medical providers to help clients."

Heather worked as a CNA before applying to medical school to become a physician. "I enjoyed working as a CNA," she said. "It definitely wasn't always (or even sometimes) glamorous, but the rewards were worth it. I loved getting to talk with patients, hear their stories. I better learned how to cope with death on the job, as it was my job to help prepare the body for the funeral home after a patient passed away. People are quite vulnerable with CNAs. They are at their worst, and their bodies are failing them. They are often dependent on you for the most basic things we often take for granted. I will be the first to tell you that my bedside manner as a physician was not developed in medical school. It was developed during my year as a CNA." Now, working as a physician, she said, "I am especially aware of the work and challenges the nurses and techs encounter as they care for my patients," she added.

Like the initial effort to gain a job working as a CNA or medical assistant, the most important components to leveraging experience in those occupations into more prestigious jobs are dedication and hard work. Maintaining a positive attitude and cheerful demeanor on the job tends to make a good impression on coworkers and employers, who make valuable connections when you want to move up the career ladder. Developing a mentor relationship with a superior in the field is beneficial in this regard, too. A trusted older person who has the job you want, or a job like the one you think you might want someday, can give you good advice and prove to be a valuable resource when it comes to advancing in the field.

Pursuing higher education in order to become eligible for an advanced career may seem intimidating. College courses are expensive and time-consuming. Once you have already set out on your career path by becoming a CNA or medical assistant, however, you may find it much more achievable than you initially thought. While these occupations won't make you rich, they pay respectably and provide money to put toward education. Some professional organizations and medical facilities offer scholarship opportunities to members or employees who are interested in earning a degree. For those who perform well while earning an associate's degree in the process of obtaining certification, some universities offer

Working as a medical assistant or certified nursing assistant can open up a variety of options in the medical field. Research and making contacts in the field may reveal unexpected opportunities.

scholarships and financial aid incentives toward completing a four-year degree. It is also possible to seek employment with a university-affiliated medical group in order to offset the cost of education.

In order to locate the best possible opportunities, keep your eyes and ears open. If you want to move up within your place of employment, look for job openings within the organization. Actively seek out chances at educational aid and job advancement, rather than waiting for them to come to you. Let your mentors know about your ambitions, so that they can pass on useful information and help you work to achieve your goals.

Finally, the importance of conducting yourself well at work cannot be emphasized enough. Every job you work is, in a way, an audition for the next job you want to attain. The people you interact with at work—your boss, your coworkers, the people you serve, everyone— can potentially affect your chances of moving up the career ladder and getting the job of your dreams. Be kind, work hard, and respect others.

GLOSSARY

AAMA American Association of Medical Assistants.

ABHES Accrediting Bureau of Health Education Schools.

ADLs Activities of daily living; term used by CNAs to encompass basic eating, grooming, and ambulatory necessities.

ambulate When referring to a patient, this means helping him or her to stand and walk with assistance.

AMT American Medical Technologists agency, offers RMA certification for medical assistants.

CAAHEP Commission on Accreditation of Allied Health Education Programs.

CCMA Certified Clinical Medical Assistant designation, offered by the National Healthcare Association.

CMA (AAMA) Certified Medical Assistant designation conferred by the Certifying Board of the American Association of Medical Assistants. The title CMA is copyrighted by the AAMA.

CNA Certified nursing assistant who administers basic care to patients and serves as a liaison to nurses.

GED General Educational Development test. Successfully completing the GED is equivalent to earning a high school diploma.

LPN Licensed practical nurse.

medical assistant A non-licensed allied health worker who performs administrative and/or clinical tasks to support the work of physicians and other health professionals.

NAHA National Association of Healthcare Assistants.

NCCT National Center for Competency Testing, offers NCMA certification for medical assistants.

NCMA National Certified Medical Assistant designation, offered by the National Center for Competency Testing.

NHA National Healthcare Assocation, offers CCMA certification for medical assistants.

NNCNA National Network of Career Nursing Assistants.

physician's assistant (PA) Unrelated and not to be confused with medical assistants, PAs complete a bachelor's degree and graduate-equivalent level accredited program to become licensed to practice medicine under the supervision of physicians and surgeons.

RMA Registered Medical Assistant designation, offered by the American Medical Technologists agency.

RN Registered nurse.

FOR MORE INFORMATION

American Association of Medical Assistants (AAMA)
20 N. Wacker Drive, Suite 1575
Chicago, IL 60606
(312) 899-1500
Web site: http://www.aama-ntl.org
The AAMA provides medical assistant professionals with
    education, certification, credential acknowledgment,
    networking opportunities, scope-of-practice protection,
    and advocacy for quality patient-centered health care.

Association of Administrative Assistants
Member-at-Large Liaison
c/o 8212 - 10 Street SW
Calgary, AB T2V 1M8
Canada
Web site: http://www.aaa.ca
This association assists members in the continuing devel-
    opment of administrative skill, underlying knowledge,
    and professional growth, thus enhancing employment
    opportunities and contributions to both workplace and
    community. Although not specific to the medical field,
    the information is applicable to administrative medical
    assistants.

Association for Healthcare Administrative Professionals
455 S. 4th Street, Suite 650
Louisville, KY 40202
(888) 320-0808
Web site: http://www.ahcap.org
This organization advances the professional development,

leadership, value, and excellence of health care administrative professionals through education, recognition, communication, and advocacy.

Canadian Medical Association
1867 Alta Vista Drive
Ottawa, ON K1G 5W8
Canada
(888) 855-2555
Web site: http://www.cma.ca
This is a national, voluntary association of physicians that advocates on behalf of its members and the public for access to high-quality health care and provides leadership and guidance to physicians.

National Association of Healthcare Assistants
501 East 15th Street
Joplin, MO 64804
(417) 623-6049
Web site: http://www.nahcacares.org
This organization works with care center administrators and nursing directors to create staff development plans to reduce turnover and improve performance among certified nursing assistants.

National Network of Career Nursing Assistants
Career Nurse Assistants Programs, Inc.
(330) 825-9342
Web site: http://www.cna-network.org
This nonprofit educational organization promotes recognition, education, research, advocacy, and peer support

development for nursing assistants in nursing homes and other long-term-care settings.

Web Sites

Due to the changing nature of Internet links, Rosen Publishing has developed an online list of Web sites related to the subject of this book. This site is updated regularly. Please use this link to access the list:

http://www.rosenlinks.com/HCC/Nurs

FOR FURTHER READING

Beaman, Nina, Lorraine Flemin-McPhillips, Kristiana Routh, and Robyn Gohsman. *Pearson's Comprehensive Medical Assisting*. New York, NY: Pearson, 2010.

Bonewit-West, Kathy. *Clinical Procedures for Medical Assistants*. Philadelphia, PA: Saunders Elsevier, 2007.

Booth, Kathryn. *Medical Assisting: Administrative & Clinical Procedures*. New York, NY: McGraw-Hill, 2010.

Brassington, Cindi, and Cheri Goretti. *MA Notes: Medical Assistant's Pocket Guide*. Philadelphia, PA: F. A. Davis Company, 2010.

Brezina, Corona. *Careers as a Medical Examiner*. New York, NY: Rosen Publishing, 2008.

Carter, Pamela J. *Lippincott's Textbook for Nursing Assistants: A Humanistic Approach to Caregiving*. Riverwoods, IL: Wolters-Kluwer/Lippincott Williams & Wilkins, 2012.

Dugan, Diana. *Successful Nursing Assistant Care*. Albuquerque, NM: Hartman Publishing, 2008.

Fields, Jennifer. *Choosing a Career as a Nurse-Midwife*. New York, NY: Rosen Publishing, 2001.

Fuzy, Jetta. *Hartman's Nursing Assistant Care: The Basics*. Albuquerque, NM: Hartman Publishing, 2010.

Hegner, Barbara, Barbara Acello, and Esther Caldwell. *Nursing Assistant: A Nursing Process Approach*. Independence, KY: Delmar, Cengage Learning, 2008.

Henderson, Beverley, and Jennifer Lee Dorsey. *Medical Terminology for Dummies*. Hoboken, NJ: Wiley Publishing, 2008.

Hosley, Julie B. *Lippincott's Pocket Guide to Medical Assisting*. New York, NY: Lippincott, 1998.

Lindh, Wilburta, Marilyn Pooler, Carol Tamparo, and
     Barbara Dahl. *Delmar's Comprehensive Medical
     Assisting: Administrative and Clinical Competencies.*
     Independence, KY: Delmar, Cengage Learning, 2009.
Moini, Jahangir. *Keys to Medical Assisting Pocket Guide.*
     New York, NY: Pearson, Prentice Hall, 2008.
Pillemer, Karl. *Nursing Assistant's Survival Guide.*
     Independence, KY: Delmar, Cengage Learning, 2013.
Rogers, Kara, ed. *Battling and Managing Disease.* New
     York, NY: Britannica/Rosen Educational Services, 2011.
Smiley, Karen. *Medical Billing and Coding for Dummies.*
     Hoboken, NJ: Wiley Publishing, 2012.
Sorrentino, Sheila, and Leighann Remmert. *Mosby's
     Textbook for Nursing Assistants.* Philadelphia, PA:
     Mosby, Elsevier, 2012.
Stein, Harold A., Rayond M. Stein, and Melvin I.
     Freeman. *The Ophthalmic Assistant: A Text for Allied
     and Associated Ophthalmic Personnel: Expert Consult.*
     Philadelphia, PA: Elsevier, 2012.

BIBLIOGRAPHY

Accrediting Bureau of Health Education Schools. "Directory of Institutions and Programs." Retrieved February 27, 2013 (https://ams.abhes.org/ams /onlineDirectory/pages/directory.aspx).

American Association of Medical Assistants. "AAMA Role Delineation Study: Occupational Analysis of the Medical Assisting Profession." 2003. Retrieved February 27, 2013 (http://www.aama-ntl.org /resources/library/aama_roledelineation2003.pdf).

American Association of Medical Assistants. "Candidate Application and Handbook for the CMA (AAMA) Certification/Recertification Examination." Retrieved February 27, 2013 (http://aama-ntl.org/resources /library/ExamApp.pdf).

American Association of Medical Assistants. "What Is a CMA (AAMA)?" Retrieved February 27, 2013 (http:// www.aama-ntl.org/about/what_is_a_cma.aspx).

American Medical Technologists. "Medical Assistant." Retrieved February 27, 2013 (http://www.american-medtech.org/Certification/MedicalAssistant.aspx).

American Medical Technologists. "Medical Assisting Task List." Retrieved February 27, 2013 (http:// www.americanmedtech.org/files/MA%20Task%20 List.pdf).

Castle, N.G., J. Engberg, R. Anderson, and A. Men. "Job Satisfaction of Nurse Aides in Nursing Homes: Intent to Leave and Turnover." *Gerontologist*, April 2007. Retrieved February 27, 2013 (http://www. ncbi.nlm.nih.gov/pubmed/17440124).

CNA Certification Programs. "The CNA Job Description and Duties." Retrieved February 27, 2013 (http://www.cnacertificationprograms.org/cna-job-description-and-duties).

CNA Certification Training. "CNA Certification Training." Retrieved February 27, 2013 (http://cnacertified training.com).

Commission on Accreditation of Allied Health Education Programs. "CAAHEP Accredited Program Search." Retrieved February 27, 2013 (http://www.caahep.org/Find-An-Accredited-Program).

Gunter, Tracy, and Nicolas Terry. "The Emergence of National Electronic Health Record Architectures in the United States and Australia: Models, Costs, and Questions." *Journal of Medical Internet Research*, March 2005. Retrieved February 27, 2013 (http://www.ncbi.nlm.nih.gov/pmc/articles/PMC1550638).

National Healthcareer Association. "Certification Process for Students." Retrieved February 27, 2013 (http://www.nhanow.com/certifications/certification-process.aspx).

National Network of Career Nursing Assistants. "How to Request Reciprocity." Retrieved February 27, 2013 (http://www.cna-network.org/questions.htm).

Phlebotomy Certification Guide. "Becoming a Certified Phlebotomist's Assistant." Retrieved February 27, 2013 (http://www.phlebotomycertificationguide.com/becoming-a-certified-phlebotomists-assistant).

Rosen, Jules. "Getting to the Bottom of CNA Turnover." *McKnight's Long-Term Care News & Assisted Living*, December 2008. Retrieved February 27, 2013 (http://www.mcknights.com/getting-to-the-bottom-of-cna-turnover/article/121691/#).

Taché, Stephanie, and Susan Chapman. "What a Medical Assistant Can Do for Your Practice." *Family Practice Management*, April 2005. Retrieved February 27, 2013 (http://www.aafp.org/fpm/2005/0400/p51.html).

U.S. Department of Labor. "Medical Assistants." *Occupational Outlook Handbook*, March 2012. Retrieved February 27, 2013 (http://www.bls.gov/ooh/healthcare/medical-assistants.htm#tab-2).

U.S. Department of Labor. "Nursing Aides, Orderlies, and Attendants." *Occupational Outlook Handbook*, April 2012. Retrieved February 27, 2013 (http://www.bls.gov/ooh/healthcare/nursing-assistants.htm#tab-4).

Ury, Allen B. "'Medical Assistant' Ranks High on U.S. News' Top 50 Job List." Everest Colleges, Institutes, and Universities, April 2012. Retrieved February 27, 2013 (http://news.everest.edu/post/2012/04/medical-assistant-ranks-high-on-top-50-job-list).

U.S. News & World Report. "Best Healthcare Jobs: Medical Assistant." Retrieved February 27, 2013 (http://money.usnews.com/careers/best-jobs/medical-assistant).

INDEX

About the Author

Jennifer Culp is an author who has worked previously as an administrative medical assistant for the East Tennessee State University Osteoporosis Center. She has also served as an editorial coordinator for the *Southern Medical Journal* and managing editor for the *Journal of Clinical Densitometry*. Currently, she writes nonfiction for young adults and children.

Photo Credits

Cover (figure) Maridav/Shutterstock.com; cover and interior pages (hospital room) Vladislav Gajic /Shutterstock.com; cover, back cover, p. 1 (background pattern) HunThomas/Shutterstock.com; pp. 4–5 (background) sfam_photo/Shutterstock.com; pp. 5 (inset), 10–11, 21, 46–47 Fuse/Thinkstock; pp. 9, 36–37 wavebreakmedia/Shutterstock.com; pp. 14–15 Monkey Business Images/Shutterstock.com; p. 16 michaeljung/Shutterstock.com; pp. 24–25 Alexander Raths/Shutterstock.com; p. 29 Steve Debenport/the Agency Collection/Getty Images; p. 31 BananaStock /Thinkstock; pp. 32, 35, 51, 66–67 © AP Images; pp. 43, 58–59 iStockphoto/Thinkstock; p. 55 Joos Mind/Stone/Getty Images; p. 60 kali9/E+/Getty Images.

Designer: Michael Moy, Editor: Bethany Bryan, Researcher: Karen Huang